LEARNING TO
BE LOVED

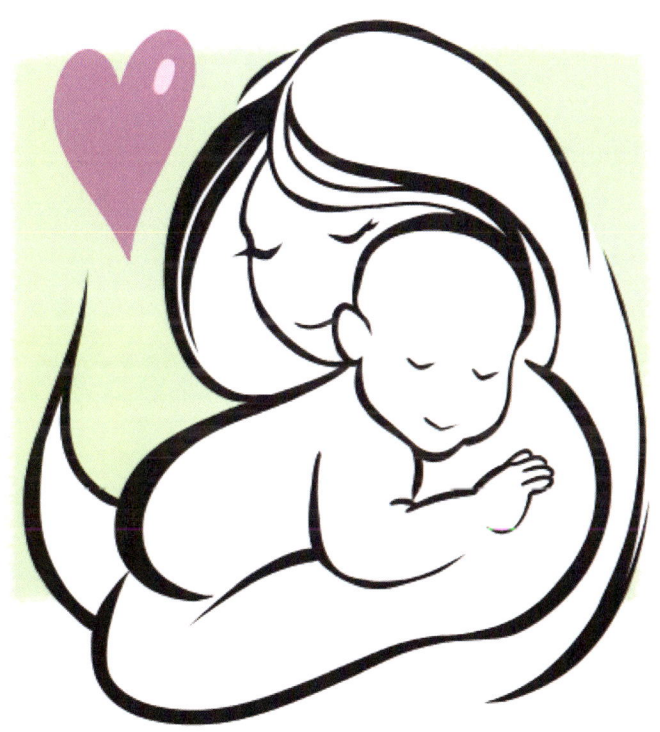

This is the story of

my daughter Layla and me.

LEARNING TO BE LOVED

A True Story of Overcoming Oppositional Defiant Disorder in an Adopted Child Using Trauma-informed Parenting

Amber Gregory

979-8-9930218-2-9 paperback
979-8-9930218-1-2 ebook

Artwork by Kayla McCoy.

For more information contact the author at LearningToBeLovedBook.com

I have presented the information in this book as truthfully and carefully as possible; the techniques I described worked for me, and they have worked for other parents, but your results may vary, depending on a variety of factors, including your consistency, dedication, and support network. I cannot and do not guarantee your success, nor is this book intended to replace professional advice from therapists, teachers, social workers, or doctors. By reading this book, you indicate your understanding that your ultimate success or failure will be the result of your own efforts, your particular situation, and innumerable other circumstances beyond my knowledge and control.

This book is dedicated to
Dr. Walter Buenning.
He gave me compassion, knowledge, hope,
and friendship. Most important of all, he gave our
beautiful family back to us. Words cannot express
the joy and gratitude I feel from knowing him.

Dear parents and caregivers,

Attachment disorders and conduct disorders are not common, but they are serious conditions. This book is not intended to tell you how to treat these disorders by yourself, without the help of a professional. I do want to give you information you need, however, to recognize the early signs. I also want to describe techniques you can do yourself that will help heal a traumatized child.

If I had recognized the signs of Reactive Attachment Disorder (RAD) and had treated it early, my daughter might not have developed more serious emotional problems. Children with trauma and attachment problems can also present with out-of-control and very naughty behavior and defiance, as seen in Oppositional Defiant Disorder (ODD), and Conduct Disorder: Childhood Onset Type (CD). If you're the parent of a child with one of these disorders, you'll probably feel overwhelmed, confused, and discouraged. Please seek help from professionals. Your local school will have psychologists and counselors who can refer you to the specialists you need.

Layla and I had a rough road in the beginning because I didn't know the signs to look for nor did I have the parenting skills to address them. If I had known, it would have saved our entire family a lot of heartache, and Layla would have healed and felt better sooner.

Would I do it all over again? You bet! The love and beauty of the relationship my daughter and I have today was so worth the struggles and time it took to heal her.

Layla and I wish all of you readers who are thinking of fostering and adopting or have already fostered or adopted a child the best of luck. Our heartfelt prayer is that you too will enjoy your healing journey as you bond together as a family.

It is the love received, not the love given, that does the healing.

Blessings,

Amber

"We delight in the beauty of the butterfly, but rarely ponder the changes it has gone through to achieve its beauty."

—Maya Angelou

As a baby grows under a mother's heart, a heart connection forms.
This is true for every baby, everywhere. Trauma happens when the bond to the mother is disrupted or broken.

8

Layla was a brand new baby. Like all babies, she was born with a *spark* inside. The *spark* was connected to her mother by a very special bond. Layla's mother took good care of her. She gave her good food. She kept her clean and dry and wrapped her in soft blankets so she was always warm. Layla's mother loved to cuddle her! Because of this love and care, Layla's *spark* ignited into a tiny flame.

9

You couldn't see it, but her flame was there, on the inside. It kept the inside of Layla's soul warm and bright. Layla was a happy baby.

Layla loved her mother. She didn't know her mother was sick. Layla thought her mother would always be there. Sadly, one day her mother wasn't there, and it broke Layla's heart.

11

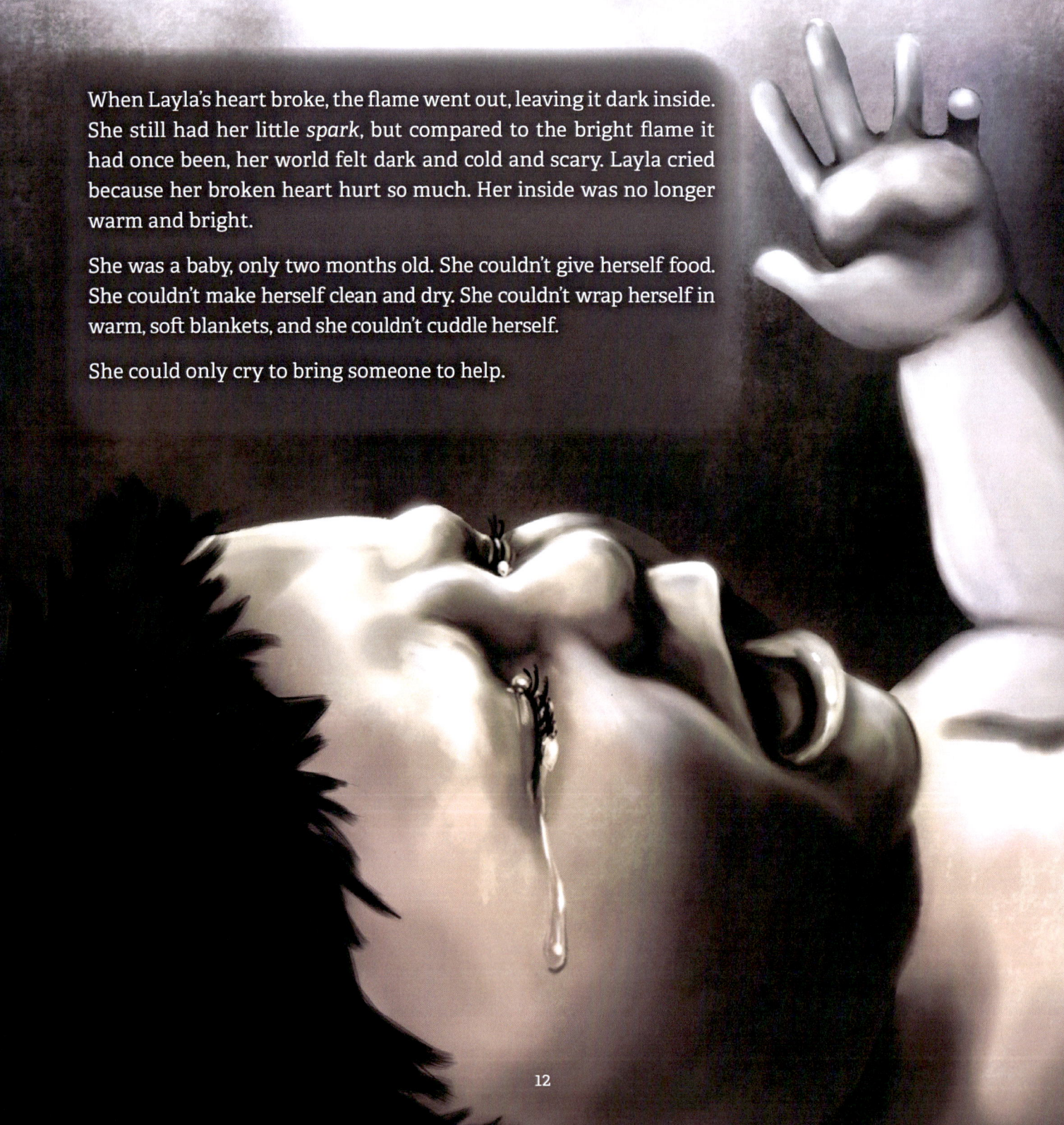

When Layla's heart broke, the flame went out, leaving it dark inside. She still had her little *spark*, but compared to the bright flame it had once been, her world felt dark and cold and scary. Layla cried because her broken heart hurt so much. Her inside was no longer warm and bright.

She was a baby, only two months old. She couldn't give herself food. She couldn't make herself clean and dry. She couldn't wrap herself in warm, soft blankets, and she couldn't cuddle herself.

She could only cry to bring someone to help.

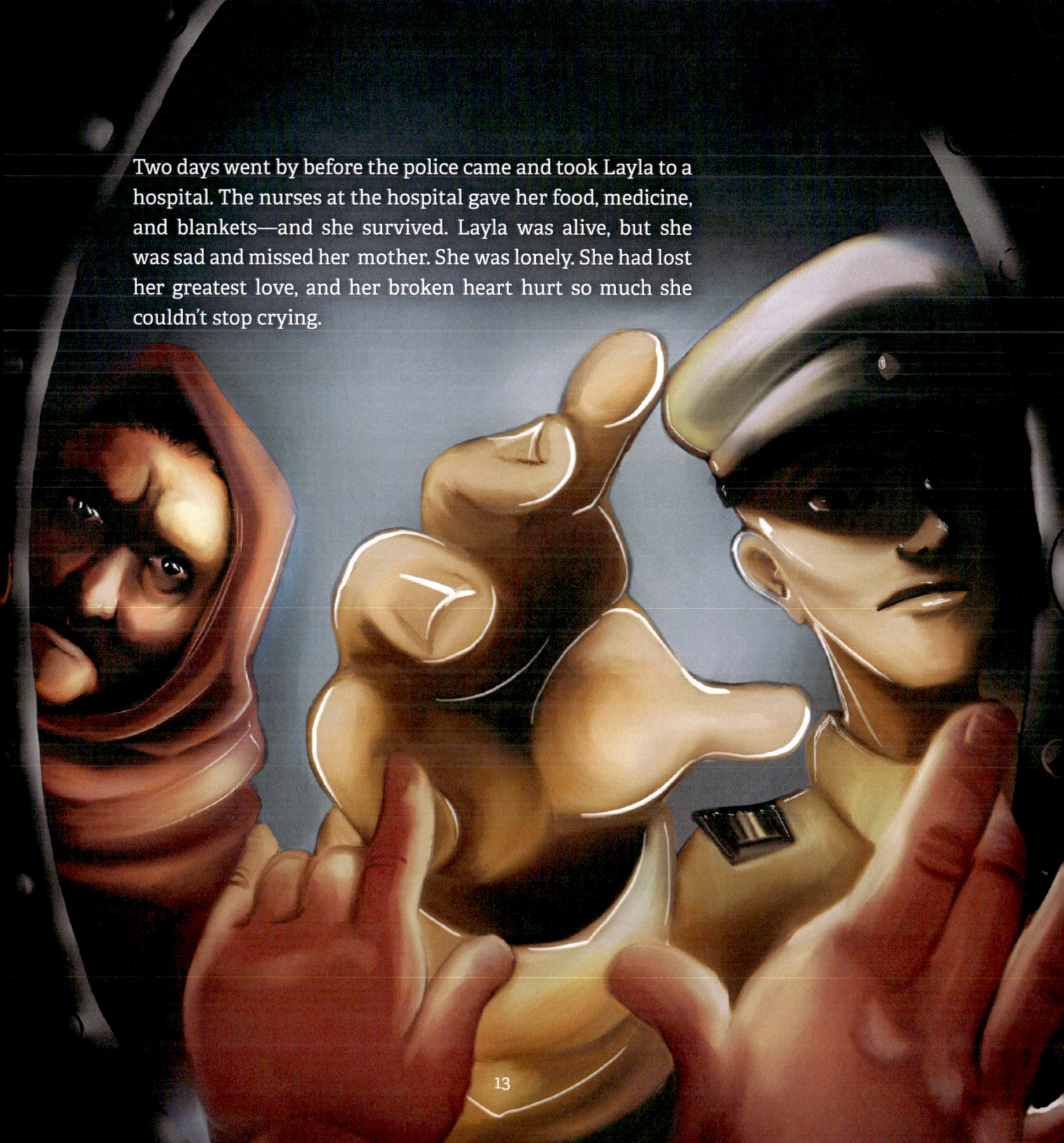

Two days went by before the police came and took Layla to a hospital. The nurses at the hospital gave her food, medicine, and blankets—and she survived. Layla was alive, but she was sad and missed her mother. She was lonely. She had lost her greatest love, and her broken heart hurt so much she couldn't stop crying.

Layla cried, but no one came to see what was wrong. No one had time to pick her up and cuddle her. She was sick too, with pneumonia. She stayed at the hospital for four months. Her cries didn't bring anyone to help, so she cried less and less. By the time she left the hospital, she only cried a little.

When she was six months old, Layla was taken to an orphanage. There were many caregivers there, but no one thought Layla was special.

Layla was at the orphanage a long time, another 18 months. She was often cold and hungry. She didn't feel good. Her tummy hurt, she couldn't breathe well, and she was lonely. The caregivers didn't feed her enough nourishing food. They didn't keep her clean or warm or dry. They did not cuddle her, comfort her, soothe her, or love her. Layla hardly ever cried now.

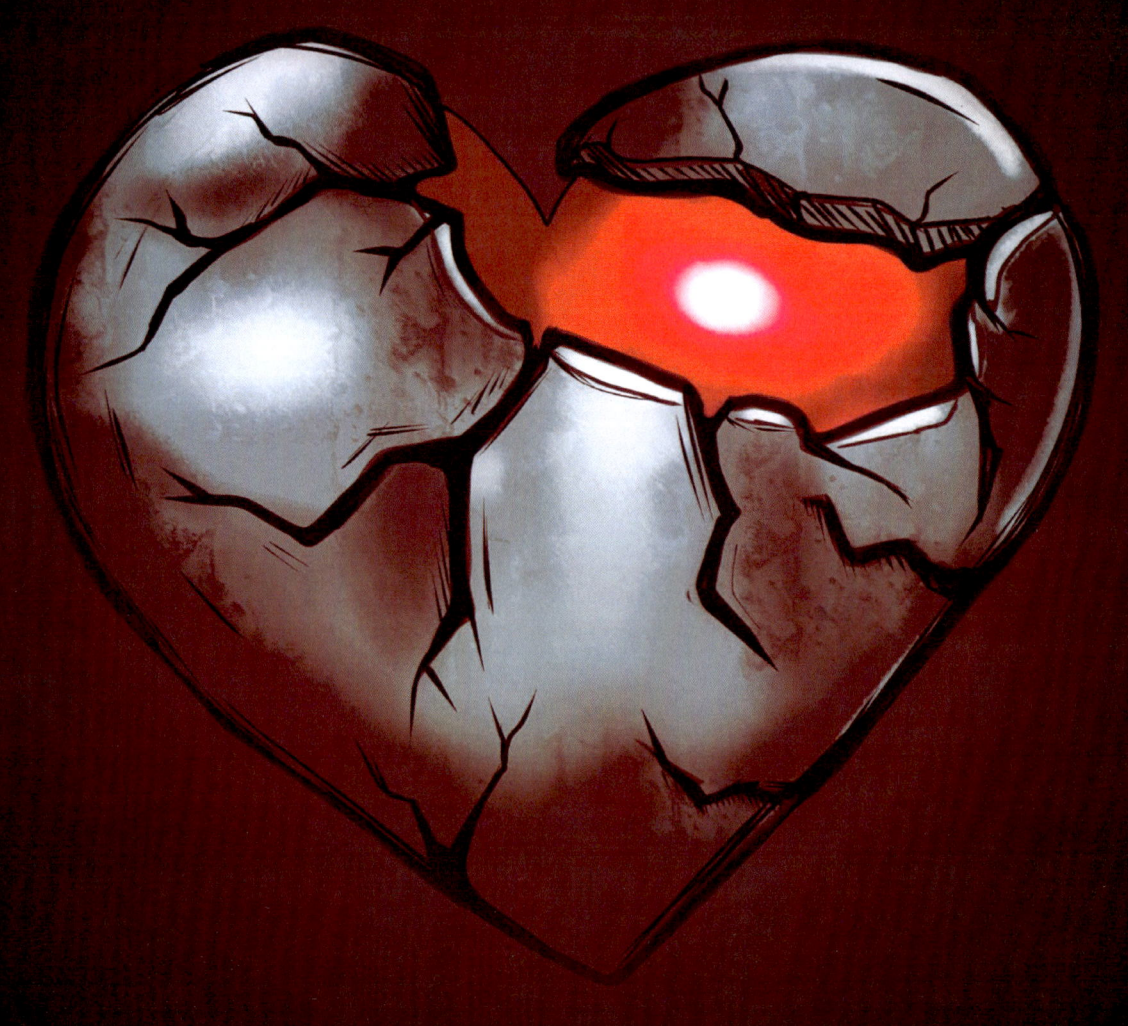

Layla had lost everything, and she couldn't even cry or get any comfort. It was so bad Layla's *spark* almost went out! She knew if her *spark* went out, she would die! So she found a way to protect her *spark*. She toughened her little heart and kept her *spark* inside of it. When she toughened her heart, she felt a little better. She felt a little safer. Every time Layla was neglected or treated cruelly or was hungry or cold, her heart grew a little tougher, and she felt a little better and a little safer. Her broken heart didn't hurt quite as much.

Even though Layla had found a way to protect her *spark*, she was still sad, hungry, and cold, and her tummy hurt. Now she never cried. No one ever picked her up, and no one ever cuddled her.

This had been going on for two years. By now, Layla wasn't doing very well. She was small. She always coughed and had a cold. Her hair was thin and had many bald spots. She couldn't walk or talk. She didn't smile or play or laugh.

Her *spark* was still there, hidden in her toughened little heart, but Layla was only a baby, and Layla needed help . . . her *spark* was starting to fade.

On the other side of the world, after giving up on hormones and surgeries, I wanted to adopt a baby. My husband agreed and after applying for adoption and taking classes, having several home studies and security checks, it was time. We were invited to meet Layla.

The day my husband and I came to see Layla, she wouldn't even look at us. We tried all day just to get her to smile. Her face stayed blank, and her body stayed rigid. We had no idea what was going on inside her, if anything! We spent all day trying to get her to look at us and get her to smile—and finally…

Layla looked at us! We smiled at Layla. When we smiled, our eyes lit up, and we tried to make Layla feel special. We kept smiling at Layla.

Tentatively, Layla smiled back!

We decided to adopt Layla and be her new mother and father!

When I adopted Layla, I knew she had special needs and had trauma in her past, but I really had no idea how much more work that was going to entail. I naively thought that with love, attention, and good food, we would have her caught up in a year. I joked that she seemed like a one-year-old, and in a year I would have a typical three-year-old.

Layla had bad allergies, which turned into pneumonia and asthma, a life-threatening condition. We were often up at night with her nebulizer, wondering if we should go to the hospital. She was very small and undernourished. The doctors called it "failure to thrive." She had speech delays and physical delays and hadn't hit the developmental milestones for many things. Later, she got diagnosed with sensory integration problems and had to wear special bifocals because of an anatomical problem with her right eye.

It seemed like there would never be a day when Layla would be healthy and play just like the other kids.

We got busy working with Layla and helping her cope with sensory problems, speech problems, and physical weakness. So much just wasn't working right!

We had concerns because she wouldn't fall asleep in our arms or if we snuggled her in with us at night.

Initially, I expected to have an adjustment period. I kept trying to gain Layla's love and was hopeful that with time she would start turning to me with her needs, that she would begin to prefer me and my husband to all other people.

During the first six months when we were all getting to know each other, I didn't worry at all because I thought that in time Layla would fit right in with our family.

At first Layla enjoyed playing with us. We took good care of Layla. We made good food for her, played with her in the bathtub, and dressed her in warm snuggly clothes.

In time, Layla started walking and saying her first words. Her very first word was "up." She would toddle over to me and say, "Up!" I would scoop her up and kiss her and snuggle her, so happy I had a little girl in my life to love!

We didn't realize that time would not cure all of her problems. Her early trauma would be a part of her for many, many years to come.

When Layla started to "light up" and walk and talk and react to attention from us and other people, this would normally indicate that she was cured of her Reactive Attachment Disorder (RAD) and failure to thrive—but because her primary bond was not healed, as she got older other emotional problems set in.

Now, Layla had Oppositional Defiant Disorder (ODD) and Conduct Disorder (CD): Childhood Onset Type.

I often picked Layla up and cuddled her and played with her. One day, something unexpected happened. I was bouncing Layla on the trampoline and we were both laughing. Layla was happy. It was then that I saw through Layla's toughened little heart and sensed . . . her *spark*! Layla felt it too. It was a powerful connection.

It was the same heart connection she knew as a brand-new baby! Feeling this connection made Layla want to cry. It was so scary she immediately tried to get away from me! The last time she had this feeling, she lost her mother, and it hurt too much. Now, instead of crying, she got angry and tried to hurt me. She dug her nails into my arm until I let go of her. She went all the way to the other side of the trampoline. She DID NOT want me touching her! She DID NOT want to cry! Most of all, she DID NOT want this connected feeling!

Having someone sense her *spark* made Layla feel really afraid.

She felt it when I connected to her *spark*, and she did not like that feeling at all! When she had a heart connection to her birth mother and lost it, she had the worst pain ever. She never wanted to feel that pain again. She knew without a doubt that her *spark* had to be protected to be safe. Her *spark* had to be protected or she would die! Therefore, without even thinking about it, she decided she would not love me, and she would keep me from loving her.

No matter what, I must never sense her *spark* again!

This was a confusing time for Layla—and her emotions made it a very confusing time for me too. Although I knew a little about Layla's early trauma, I felt like her life started when I adopted her. I thought with good food and positive attention and love, Layla would bond, blossom, and grow.

When Layla couldn't block all the love going into her, and her toughened little heart softened enough for me to make a heart connection with her, I believe this scared her down to her core, at an unconscious level. It made her so uncomfortable she set about blocking my love. If I turned up the loving feelings and tried to pour more love into her, she would go to greater lengths to block my love.

I believe she felt she was protecting herself. She had protected herself in the past so well that she was able to survive a life-and-death situation at the orphanage, a situation I would never want to endure. But along the way, she damaged her heart. In keeping her *spark* in, she kept love out. We all need love to grow healthy—but she didn't know that. She just knew that my love didn't feel safe. She felt safer when I wasn't loving her. So the best way to feel safe was to make sure I didn't actively try to love her. That led to a greater divide of emotions. Layla pushed me away in all kinds of ways.

It kind of makes sense.

This was the beginning of my self-doubt and Layla eliciting that feeling in me. I started to worry.

As we progressed from sign language to single words and from crawling to walking and then to therapeutic horseback riding. Layla became more defiant and started breaking things. Well, she was two and a half, I told myself; it's the terrible two's after all.

By age three, Layla would not eat the food I made her. She also wouldn't sleep at night. She snuck out of her bedroom and got into drawers and cupboards that were off-limits. Once, when I wasn't paying attention, Layla hurt our family dog. Once, when I wasn't paying attention, Layla tried to kill my rabbit!

This made me really scared and very, very worried.

Then as she turned three and a half . . . well she didn't have tantrums, but she certainly didn't comply. She sneaked around, hurt our pets, damaged walls, broke toys, and ruined her clothes. This was all done with not too much expression on her face, which made the whole thing somehow scarier. We thought she was acting out.

As Layla turned four, my mother finally confirmed my fears: the problem was my fault. "She seems fine with the rest of us, Amber. Unfortunately, not all personalities mesh well. I'm sorry, honey, there's nothing wrong with her ... you just don't click."

33

By the time Layla was four and a half, I felt worried almost all the time. I was so worried about Layla that I told people what was happening. Everyone said Layla seemed healthy and happy … and it was true. She was happy with other people. She sat on her teachers' laps. She behaved well for her grandma.

I was scared and getting very tired. I felt really sad and rejected that Layla didn't seem to want me as a mommy. I started to get depressed.

How many ways did Layla push my love away?

Layla broke her toys, she peeled her wallpaper, and she wet the bed every night. Layla flooded our bathroom; she drew pictures of me being dead. She wouldn't ever hold my hand while walking, even in the parking lots where she had to in order to be safe. She also scared me by wrapping cords around her neck. I started getting angry. I started yelling. I stopped cuddling Layla. When I stopped cuddling Layla, she relaxed, because if I was angry, I couldn't sense her *spark* and make that loving heart connection. Layla felt better. She thought if she could keep her *spark* protected, she would be okay. She spent every day trying to make me angry, scared, worried, unhappy, rejected, and sad.

She knew if I stayed angry, scared, worried, unhappy, rejected, and sad, I couldn't truly love her.

One day, Layla sneaked scissors out of a kitchen drawer. While I was talking on the phone, she cut off a hunk of my hair.

36

Still, I kept trying to pick Layla up and cuddle her—but every time, she pushed me away with her bad behavior. I was confused and felt there was something wrong, but when I asked her pediatrician, he said Layla was fine. Layla was walking and talking and growing. The doctor said I was doing a great job taking care of Layla.

Still, I was worried. I knew something was wrong. I just knew it.

During the time Layla was two and a half to when she was four and a half, I slowly got sadder and angrier as she pushed my love away by acting naughty. I kept telling doctors and therapists that I thought there was something wrong.

And I was right! When Layla toughened her little heart, she damaged it. She was trying to keep her *spark* in, but she ended up keeping love out. All babies and children need love to grow strong, healthy, and happy. She had made such a toughened little heart that she was starving herself of love.

One day the police came to the house.

Layla had told her teacher that her father had hurt her. She was very convincing, and the teacher called the police. Her father had not hurt Layla, but there was an investigation. My husband and I were scared. We didn't know if they would take Layla and her brother away from us. What if my husband had to go to jail? Or what if our friends or members of our church found out and believed Layla's story? My husband and I could barely believe that our own daughter could destroy our family with such an untrue story.

During the investigation, professionals confirmed that Layla had an attachment disorder, and my husband was cleared of all charges. The police didn't take the children away, but now I was scared and angry and wary. After almost three years of my disconnected emotional relationship with Layla, I started to feel so unhappy, angry, and depressed—and now scared—that I wasn't sure I wanted to be Layla's mother anymore.

Meanwhile, the more upset I got, the better Layla seemed to feel. I never felt her *spark* or made a heart connection now. I believe that made Layla feel safe.

"The most beautiful things
in the world cannot be seen
or even touched,
they must be felt with the heart."

—Helen Keller

Trust your instincts.

Mothers are almost always the ones reporting,

"I think there is something wrong."

Not one person, no one from our adoption agency or our social worker for our home study, not all the therapists in and out of our house, not our pediatrician, not any of our friends who had also adopted children—no one at all told us the signs were there. Along with parasites, allergies, asthma, pneumonia, sensory integration problems, and really too many issues to count, Layla had emotional problems as well.

Because the developmental stages of young children can be varied and hard to read, at first, we passed off her behaviors as being due to her early deficiencies. We thought she was resilient and would catch up and settle in eventually. But we were wrong.

Like most problems, the earlier you identify and treat the situation, the better the outcome.

When Layla was five, we hired Dr. Walter Buenning (Dr. B) who taught us about Reactive Attachment Disorder (or RAD—and what today would be diagnosed as Oppositional Defiant Disorder and Conduct Disorder: Childhood Onset Type). He also taught us new parenting techniques to help heal Layla by getting unhealthy control away from her, putting us back in charge of our household, and finding ways to get her to receive our love. The next few pages are some of his teachings about parenting techniques, as well as some things I picked up on my own along the way.

Love and Limits

*"It's our love that gives our children
the ability to soar high on the trapeze,
and it is our limits or rules which
let them know there is a net below
them and that they are safe."*

—Dr. Walter Buenning

**Next to food,
what a baby needs most
is a mother's love.**

As a parent, your environment should provide your children with everything a pregnant mother's body did: safety, nourishment, and love. A parent takes care of a new baby's needs up to fifty times per day: feeding, burping, rocking, changing diapers, talking, and tickling. Every time a need is met, the bond between parent and child strengthens. This is called the attachment cycle.

The Attachment Cycle

Think of a newborn baby's attachment cycle like a clock. The cycle goes around and around many times in a newborn's day—but as an adopted mom or foster mom of an older child, you may have to create ways to attach throughout the day. Keeping your young child with you and interacting with play and puzzles is a great way to do this, but don't underestimate incorporating your child's help with jobs. Pairing socks as you fold laundry, adding carrots to the soup pot, folding napkins, feeding the dog or cat, and sitting on your lap while you take time to cuddle are good ways to strengthen the bond.

It is not the love we give our children that matters so much as the love they receive that binds them to us. In other words, no matter how full our hearts may be with love for our children, it won't do our children any good unless we can find ways to persuade them to accept our love. A child with a strong bond will feel safe and stop trying to defy you at every turn.

Don't worry about your child learning colors or letters. Let the teachers do that. Your job is getting that bond working. You are the only one who can do that. Make it your first priority.

The Attachment Cycle

0 months to 36 months

Examples of attaching with a newborn:

- Baby is hungry, parent feeds baby, need is met (the bond strengthens).
- Baby has wet diaper, parent changes it, need is met (the bond strengthens).
- Baby cries, parent picks up and cuddles baby, need is met (the bond strengthens).

In one day the attachment cycle has gone around many times.

Let's pretend every time the cycle goes around we will put one quarter in the child's emotional piggy bank.

We have all seen kids who are "emotionally rich" and those who are "emotionally poor."

Sometimes the trauma of the loss of a birth mother or the trauma of abuse and neglect will make a child choose not to accept a new mother's or father's love. In effect, the child will block "quarters" from going into their emotional piggy bank, and they will look "quarter poor."

Once again, it's the love received, not the love that is given that matters.

Reactive Attachment Disorder is similar to anorexia.

People with anorexia choose not to eat, not because they don't like the food, but because they don't want to take the food inside. A child with RAD doesn't push the love away because they don't like the kind of love they are getting, but because they don't want the love inside.

When a person with anorexia has not eaten and collapses, you need to feed them with an IV first—then treat the underlying disorder. With RAD or CD (conduct disorder) children must get love in first and then work on the underlying disorder.

A child with RAD will not "spontaneously attach." You must intervene to help the child form an attachment.

49

There are two distinct parts of effective parenting: getting love in and getting your child to obey your rules. You absolutely need both. Your child needs to accept your love, and your child needs to trust your authority and accept your rules. If you skip either part, you will not have a successful outcome.

 It was harder for me to do the rules—so I'm going to start with them and how you can get your child to obey them.

Emotional Safety = Feeling Safe and Calm

Learning to obey the rules is very important to a child's feeling of safety. When we talk about rules, there are both external rules and then the internal structure that those external rules help develop. There are external rules at both home and school, and those rules help with internalizing and creating an internal structure. Internal structure equals emotional safety. Emotional safety means you feel safe and calm. We want our children feeling safe and calm so they grow up to be happy, healthy, self-reliant adults. They need to have good internal structures to do this. They need to know right from wrong so they can do right instead of wrong.

Be careful, though, that you don't end up working so hard to get your child to obey that you become unloving, harsh, controlling, or vindictive. The minute you are unloving, you are on the path to your child hardening their heart. Remember, your child has been hurt, and that is why it is hard for them to trust you.

Sit-by-Me (learning to obey your rules)

Get used to saying, "Come sit by me," with a smile in *your* heart. When children are misbehaving, have them sit by you. Of course children may not meekly follow and sit. You have to get them into a designated area by you, and then just wait them out. Do not engage with them. This is "time-in," not time-out. They need to take this time to get themselves together.

They are learning to calm themselves. They are learning to reorganize themselves. They are building a good internal structure. It takes time. When they're ready, they will sit calmly for about two to three minutes. You'll be able to tell by the expression on their face when their heart has softened and they are ready to obey your rules again. Then you, because you are in charge, tell them they are done.

Obeying your rules is all about trusting you. That is why it is a foundation for a healthy attachment.

Think of Layla's "toughened heart" as a divided heart—one part is attached and another part is unattached. Attachment disorders have different severities.

There are times when the child is living in their attached heart and they will be compliant and loving. At other times, they will be living in their unattached heart and will exhibit bad behaviors, such as being destructive, spitting, sneaking, hiding knives or scissors in their rooms, and hurting themselves, animals, and other children—and so on.

You will need to get love inside both parts to help them heal.

Bind Them with Your Love

Just as following rules is important, it's also crucial for them to trust you enough that they let you lovingly take care of them. In short, it is imperative that your child receives your love. In Layla's case, we tried loving her in typical ways, like playing together, softly rubbing her back, brushing her hair, lightly touching her face, playing piggy-toe games, playing peek-a-boo, gentle tickling, dancing together, singing together, or just having her snuggle in at TV time. Mostly she didn't like any of this from me, although she allowed it with other people, even strangers. With me, she would ignore me or act so naughty I would oftentimes get angry and stop.

After I knew what was wrong, I hung in there. Even if Layla would pull away from me, I would insist she let me spend time brushing her hair or drawing on her back until she relaxed. If she thrashed about and tried to spit or bite, I would wrap her in a special mat the occupational therapist gave us. We had been instructed on how to use it because Layla had not been held and cuddled enough as a baby, so the mat worked to swaddle her and help her organize her brain with her body. It was meant to reteach her brain to like the comforting feeling of someone holding her. The mat was never wrapped around her head. It went from the shoulders down, so we could see her face. We also had to be careful it didn't hurt her or restrict her breathing in any way.

It was pretty crazy at first. Layla would get really mad and spit and then laugh manically, while I would hold her with this mat around her and say comforting things. Eventually, she would visibly relax . . . and cry. This was the little girl who never ever cried! She would cry, and I would rock her in her mat, and she would let me. This cuddly time was mandatory, and we did it every day.

I also spent time "babying" her every day. I let her drink with a bottle in my lap, wrapped in a blanket, while I rocked her gently and talked to her sweetly. This was a perfect way to get love in even before she healed much.

And a word of advice—invest in a rocking chair. You will spend many hours rocking your child, which helps soothe their nerves as well as your own.

Eventually, instead of the therapy mat, I used a soft fluffy blanket, and after a long while, I could just hold her with my bare arms, although she still preferred the blanket.

Just like your "sit by me," you do this as long as it takes for your child to settle down and accept your love.

56

Mandatory Cuddly Time/Containment

If your child acts aggressively and tries to bite, kick, scratch, and pull away from you, you may have to contain them. The number-one rule in doing so is that the child never gets hurt. You must have control of your child in a way that means you are loving and caring, and they do not get hurt. Not getting hurt means no bruises, no red marks, no scratches, no strained joints, and no restricted breathing.

A child thrashing about trying to bite, kick, and scratch can hurt themselves. You must not let this happen. That is why you control their body and head. This is very uncomfortable for them emotionally, and they will probably fight you initially.

We did this with Layla until she gave in and cried or relaxed, but you can decide to do this for twenty to thirty minutes and then stop. Do what feels right for you. But it is absolutely essential to have your child allow you to cuddle and hold them, and if they choose to fight it, then you must contain them as lovingly and as gently as you can. This is a necessary step in their healing, their trusting you, and their letting love into their toughened little hearts.

When Layla stopped fighting, she cried. Then I was able to stroke her hair and soothe her.

For this kind of mandatory loving time, the parent providing it must be in a one hundred percent loving and caring place. If your annoyance or anger gets triggered, your overtures of love can quickly start to get punitive, and there will be no healing. Being wrapped in a mat to reorganize can become being *trapped in a mat,* with the child feeling like they are fighting for their lives.

If you are somewhere that you cannot wrap your child in a therapy blanket, you can hold them in your arms, but be very careful not to hurt them.

It took years for Layla to allow and actually enjoy me loving and cuddling her, but we got there in the end. After she got cuddled in her mat or blanket, her behavior improved. Getting her to receive my love helped her to be in her "attached heart." At first the good behavior only lasted an hour or so. But as time went on, we got a day or two out of her. Then a week. Then most of a month. Eventually, there were many more good days than bad days. I like to think of the timeline of Layla's healing like a corkscrew. It was slow and sometimes felt like it didn't move at all. But when I looked back in time, I could see the progress. We were on a path to an eventual end. It was just slow and none of us knew when we would get there.

You are in it to win it! Control what you can—
your heart, your words, your touch, and your intentions.

Layla needed:
my love to be stronger than her hurt.

I was Layla's mother, and if she'd had cancer or diabetes, you'd better believe I would've been there as her rock to depend on and to help her heal. Committing to healing her early trauma was no different.

61

Layla needed:
me to see through her naughty actions
to the toughened, heartbroken child inside.

When Layla was afraid of letting love in, she behaved very naughty!

Layla needed:
my commitment and purpose
to be stronger than her remembrance of loss.

When we first met Layla, she couldn't walk or talk. She had bald spots from being left in a crib and a chronic tummy ache from parasites and being hungry. She was very neglected, sad, and profoundly lonely. She no longer cried because no one came to help her.

Layla needed:
me to be more determined that she would love, trust, and obey
than she was determined to push me away and stay sick.

Tell your child what is true! Be sure you mean what you say with your whole being . . .

"You need love from me, like you need healthy food."

"I love you and you need to learn to trust me."

"I will be here for you and I will keep you."

"I want you to be healthy and safe."

"I'm your mommy, and I will help you."

Things you may encounter with a child who has experienced trauma:

- Self-injurious behavior (SIB)
- Unhealthy control
    - Triangulation of adults
    - Sibling retaliation
    - Lying
    - The "dumb act" (feigned helplessness)
- Danger to your pets' safety
- Poor performance at school
- Bed-wetting
- Prowling at night
- Swearing, spitting, screaming, nose picking
- Trauma triggers
- Teaching respect (making restitution)
- Understanding what's "fair" in new ways
- Bad days
- Discipline issues (no spanking!)
- Homeschooling? (it depends)
- Illness
- A need for babying (reparenting)
- A lack of resiliency
- Challenges required for a good prognosis
- Shame

Unhealthy Control

Dependency is at the heart of attachment. Every child depends on caregivers, and this need is inescapable. But when caregivers are neglectful, abusive, or emotionally absent, children often avoid dependency and fight for control to survive.

Layla's story shows this clearly. A caregiver once called her a "clever baby" because she knew which infants she could steal food from. By age two, she had learned that crying would not bring help. Instead, she became hypervigilant—constantly scanning who, what, when, and how to take food. To survive, she met her own needs or went hungry.

Layla wasn't just reluctant to depend on us; she was terrified. As Dr. B explained, parents are meant to "fly the plane" that carries children safely into adulthood. Traumatized children, however, try to seize the cockpit, showing their need for control through defiance—sometimes loud, sometimes quiet.

This struggle for control comes from fear and lack of trust, not defiance for its own sake. These children are doing the best they can with limited tools. Still, they lack the skills to "fly their plane." Even when they gain control, anxiety grows.

That's why parents must remain steady at the controls. Loving guidance and firm but gentle limits help children feel safe enough to trust. Healing takes time, patience, and commitment, but with love and consistency, children can learn to let go of fear and move toward wholeness.

"Giving unhealthy control to an unwell child is like giving alcohol to an alcoholic." —Dr. B

Most children do not question the rightness of adults being in charge. In fact, it will cause a lot of anxiety if they are put into a situation of too much responsibility.

A child with trauma has had an adult crash their plane, maybe more than one adult, and they try hard to get in the cockpit and fly their own plane. If they are in control and have gotten into the cockpit you will have endless battles of defiance. They wear you down! Also, a child who is "flying the plane," doesn't have time to learn numbers, colors, how to tie their shoes, their classmate's names, etc.

Just remember, you are "flying the plane" and you have to get them out of the cockpit and accept your rules; they need to accept that they are a dependent child and they can trust you. When they trust you, they can feel safe, and that is when they will start doing well at school, keeping their hands washed, and helping prepare dinner as a fun way to spend time with you. The seemingly endless control issues cease, and your child and you start enjoying spending time together.

Triangulation of Adults

This is hard to detect and another form of unhealthy control. It basically means that some unwell children are quite skilled at playing the adults in their life against each other—you and your husband, you and the teacher, you and their grandma, you and the babysitter, etc. Family counseling and talk therapy will *not* work in this situation. Usually, the counselor will end up trying to "help" the mother by addressing her problems, and that is just what the child wants. If you are sorting out conflicts with your spouse, the teacher, and Grandmom, then your child is not healing. It is imperative you have the support of your family, and that they side with you. They may not believe your child is really the problem, and they may harbor doubts about your assessment. Do not let this happen. All the adults in your child's life must be on the same page, trusting your insight and judgement. Believe in yourself and be firm!

Sibling Retaliation

A word on siblings: your unwell child may be very good at getting unhealthy control, and it is pretty easy for them to control their siblings. For example, one day our son came inside crying like crazy that Layla had killed a caterpillar. Layla quietly turned the story around, and within a minute, our son started saying he had killed the caterpillar. After getting to the bottom of it, we realized Layla had her brother lying for her. Although her brother lied for her, he later got upset that he got blamed for something he didn't do. Then he retaliated. Welcome to a house where things are in uproar, and you are frazzled!

In addition to "stirring the pot" like this to keep things in emotional uproar, some unwell children like to control younger siblings or other vulnerable children as a way of acting out the harm done to them. In this way, the unwell child feels more in control. It's very important to not let other children be harmed while healing is taking place.

Lying

If your child can lie to you and get away with it, they have gained some unhealthy control. It's very important that you don't let things slide. Notice when they are lying to you, and call them on it, every time. Letting things slide leads to them having unhealthy control. They will not trust an adult they can "snow."

When Layla started kindergarten, our progress at home came to a screeching halt. I couldn't figure out what changed. I was discouraged and redoubled my efforts at home, but still the defiant behavior reared its head. She was hoarding food, tearing her clothing, and so on. I thought maybe it was just the big change of going to school, or maybe she just needed time to adjust.

One day I asked Layla's teacher if she could use any help. She said, "Sure!" and I found out exactly why my new parenting techniques stopped working. When I entered the classroom and saw Layla, I immediately knew something was going on. Her hair, which I insisted she keep neatly pulled away from her face, had been pulled out of its holder and was wild and in her face. She had a vacant "dumb" expression on her face.

I went to her and knelt down, looked her right in the eye, and said quietly and not angrily but sternly, "You might be fooling your teacher, but I know exactly what you are doing. Fix your hair and wipe that look off your face." She did both. I gave her a smile and hugged her.

I continued helping out in the class for a while and watched Layla interact with the other kids and her teacher. Everything seemed okay, so I thought maybe I had figured out what was wrong, but near the end of class, the kids had to put an art project out in the hall to dry. When it was Layla's turn to go out into the hall, I watched her fumble at the door handle, making quite a show of looking confused and helpless.

> "You have to be more perceptive than your child can be deceptive."

Her project started listing sideways as she looked searchingly around the room. Another little girl hopped up. "Oh, Layla! I'll help you!" This kind soul came to Layla's rescue and opened the door and held it for her. I smiled at the girl and asked her name. She told me and said proudly that she always helped Layla because Layla was too weak to open doors by herself. I raised an eyebrow at Layla.

"Layla, can you please show Libby how you can open the door by yourself?"

Layla hopped to, turned the knob, and opened the door like a champ.

"Thank you so much, Libby, for helping Layla," I said, "but from now on it's really important that Layla do it for herself."

Layla had a lot of unhealthy control in that situation. When she got away with it, her healing stopped. Her behavior started back on track that very afternoon after school. Yep, I just had to be more perceptive than she was being deceptive. I also had to stop her "snowing" the other children with her feigned helplessness. Mostly, I had to get her out of the cockpit so I could get busy flying the plane.

The "Dumb Act"
(Feigned Helplessness)

The dumb act or feigned helplessness is a passive-aggressive way that unwell children try to gain unhealthy control. It is a crazy-making behavior that needs to be nipped in the bud. This can take many forms.

One time, Layla flooded my bathroom, and when I told her to clean it up, she pretended she couldn't understand my instructions. When I handed her a towel, she used the corner to gently dab at the enormous puddle, which really set me off.

Your child may also be giving you a form of the dumb act by saying, "What?" and making you repeat yourself several times, or the inverse of that, where they answer you so quietly you are saying, "What?" while bending closer and closer to hear them.

Layla also often acted helpless in front of my relatives or my friends. She frequently acted like she couldn't lift or carry things when she could. Sometimes she pretended she couldn't put caps on bottles or open containers. She would look around beseechingly until someone came to her rescue and helped her.

In general, I would suggest if your child is doing something that is bugging you, ask them to stop. If they insist on being "dumb," have them sit by you in a "time-in" until they are ready with their good sitting to snap out of it.

In short, if you are feeling at all annoyed, assume they are messing with you, and take the control back.

How do you know when to give kids heathy control?

Only when they have the skill, knowledge, judgment, and self-control to handle it. Then they get a little more privilege and responsibility.

Never just because they want it.

Never just by age.

Never because other kids their age are allowed to.

Healthy control keeps your child in a curious state of interest to learn and accomplish new tasks. Unhealthy control means they are not ready for the new responsibility and thus will have anxiety about being able to handle it.

Anxiety Principle:

"Whenever we have more responsibility than ability, we will get anxious."

–Dr. B

Anxious children will behave in naughty ways until you notice they have more than they can handle. Very anxious children may harm themselves to distract themselves from their uncomfortable emotions. This is often the root cause of self-injurious behavior (SIB).

Self-Injurious Behavior (SIB)

As a young child, Layla would wrap cords, scarves, strings, or anything long and skinny around and around her neck. This behavior scared the heck out of me. If I turned my back for a minute while she was in the bathtub, she would crank the hot water and stand in the stream, causing her skin to turn an angry red.

In older children, hurting themselves might also include cutting, being promiscuous, doing drugs, or drinking alcohol, as well as physically hurting themselves in other ways.

Even though with time, things kept getting better and better, this was one issue I found out about the hard way. Layla started cutting herself after I thought our problems were behind us, when she was twelve years old. I took her to a psychiatrist, and he recommended talk therapy for her. She wasn't a little girl anymore, and it was time for her to learn about her reactions and what she could do to feel better in healthy ways.

Your Pets' Safety

All of my stories in the book are true. Layla really did hurt our family dog, and she really did almost kill my rabbit. Thank goodness I caught her in time, because losing a pet would have been really hard for me to forgive. Some children with trauma in their past just aren't well enough to feel compassion for an animal. Also, hurting pets is perfect for upsetting adults and children in the home. Soon after the incident, I re-homed all my rabbits. If Layla was at home, I kept our sturdily built golden retriever right with me. Our cat wouldn't go near her with a ten-foot pole, so we let him take care of himself.

It is sad to lose a pet by re-homing, but until your child heals substantially, it is better that the animal be safe. I believe your child will love animals some day; think of how much guilt and remorse they will feel if they had permanently harmed or killed one of the family pets. Actually, Layla was extremely upset when she read that part of this book. She didn't remember being cruel to animals. She really loves animals now and is very kind to them.

Poor Performance at School

This may be hard to hear, but if your unwell child is doing poorly at school, don't worry about it. When they heal, they will probably like learning and catching up. Let the school worry about academic performance. You have a more important job. The bond your child makes with you will help them be able to bond with others. Being able to connect to others with their hearts will be far more valuable in their lives. They will have healthy friendships and healthy love relationships. In the end, what most people want is a special connection to another living being.

A healthy bond means your child is not defying you and others at every turn. So they can relax their hyper-vigilant state and start getting curious, and then the learning will take place as it should.

To work on this at home you should do "jobs" together. Have your child help you. They can fold towels, pair socks, weed the garden, do workbooks, help cook, and so on. Any job that they do and follow through on is a drop in the bucket to them obeying the rules and trusting your authority. This also means they are accepting their role as a dependent child in the household and not trying to fly the plane.

Any time your child practices trust, that is time well spent!

Bed-Wetting

Another big problem Layla had was bed-wetting. I'm not talking when she was two and three, when you might expect that. I'm talking she took her pull-up off at night and wet the bed even when she was older. I tried rubber pants, I tried limiting water after 6:00 pm, I tried putting her zip-up pajamas on backwards. She didn't occasionally wet the bed; she removed her pull-up and wet the bed *every night.* Sometimes the first whiff of pee when I opened her bedroom door in the morning would irk me.

It is very common for children who have trauma in their past to wet the bed. It may take a long while to get rid of this problem because the children don't want to give it up. Children do not do a 'sit-by-me' for bed wetting. This is not defiance.

The best way to handle it is to have the child strip their pee-soaked bed, go in the laundry room with everything that is soiled, and put everything into the washer with soap. When it's finished, the child puts it in the dryer. When it's dry, the child can make the bed and be ready for bedtime. The focus should always be on the wet items not being sanitary. You want the child to stay healthy, and that is why their bedding has to be cleaned for the next night. The child is never "bad" for wetting the bed and does not do a "time-in" for bed-wetting. Just keep the cleaning tedious, and make sure they know it's their responsibility. It took Layla from age five when we started this technique to age eleven, when she finally stopped bed-wetting. Was I sometimes irritated or tired by it? Or did I try to plead with her to stop? Yes. When she was ten, I even asked her pediatrician to prescribe pills to help stop the bed-wetting; they didn't work. I started to think of it differently, and that helped. If Layla could endure her early trauma, then I could help her clean up the residual mess it made. It was worth the effort it took to both keep her in clean bedding and let her know she was loved and didn't have to tackle problems alone anymore.

Prowling

The answer to this one: put an alarm on the bedroom door.

Layla liked to prowl at night, which led to sleeplessness for her and me. It is unsafe (and illegal) to lock a child in their bedroom. Instead, we installed an alarm up high, so when we tucked her in and turned it on, she would set it off if she opened the door. She tested it a few times, but ended up going to sleep. Also, it is so sad, but before your child came to live with you, it's possible they were abused at night by adults or other children. The alarm assures them of a safe place to rest.

Don't underestimate good rest for the entire family. It led to better choices for Layla and me. Layla learned a healthy boundary and that she was "safe and secure."

Swearing, Spitting, Screaming, Nose-Picking

There are some problems, like bed-wetting, you may run into that are not feasible or effective to make children sit for. Another option is to "prescribe the problem." Swearing, nose-picking, spitting, screaming, or other habitual behaviors are good examples of behaviors you want to stop in your child, but can be more effectively addressed this way, than by using a "time-in" or a "sit-by-me."

Here is what you do. Don't get exasperated or upset. Just tell the child you understand they are wanting to do that behavior and designate a spot you will allow it. You have then brought them and their behavior somewhat under your authority or rules.

Be understanding. "Layla, I see that you really want to spit and play in it." (This is an actual problem we had for many months.) "So I'm going to let you sit in the kitchen in this small area and you can spit and play in it until you don't want to anymore. Then you can use dish soap, water, and a sponge to clean it all up. I will help you get your dirty clothes off and washed, and then you can clean off your face and hands."

For swearing or screaming, they may be allowed to do so in their bedroom with the door shut until they don't want to anymore. Again, you have then brought them somewhat into the circle of your rules and authority.

You will feel less angry or repulsed by a behavior you have now taken charge of and allowed within your parameters.

Trauma Triggers

Try to remember that attachment problems are more likely to occur in children who have also been abused or neglected. Anybody abused or neglected who has lost their mother is going to need a calm, safe place to heal. Limiting TV, video games, and loud music will help them be calm and make it easier to bond. Consider too that many of these children didn't get a proper babyhood. I would be very careful about allowing them to see anything bloody or violent. I would even be careful squishing bugs.

When Layla was three, we found out that she liked to fish, so we took her fishing several times in the summer. When she was five, the people next to us had a fish swallow a hook and when they pulled it out, the insides came out with it. Thinking it was kind of gross but interesting, I let Layla take a look. She spent the rest of the day quiet and distant and quite odd.

Trauma triggers can happen any time after a person has a traumatic event. Be very mindful of what may be triggering your child and try to get them to a quiet, safe place and help them cope.

Teaching Respect (Making Restitution)

Layla never really felt sorry for several years. So we focused on her making restitution rather than saying a word that had no meaning. So, if she put a hole in the wall, she had to clean it up and pay me back by helping me do the dishes or clean my shoes or something. She had to understand she was making up to me for what she did.

This is super important with siblings as well, so that the sibling doesn't get hard feelings and retaliate. Of course, if a sibling wrongs your unwell child, that child will make restitution.

If, for example, you slip up and don't pay attention to where the dog is, and your child hurts the dog, have them gently brush the dog, under your supervision, to tell the dog they understand they shouldn't have done that. In the beginning, your child may not feel sorry at all. They might have enjoyed hurting the dog or breaking their brother's toy. But they need to pay restitution and hopefully understand there are direct consequences for their actions. If they refuse to make restitution, they can sit by you in a "time-in" until they are ready to do it.

We started Layla making restitution around age five, but it was about two and a half years before she actually felt remorse for doing something bad that hurt someone else.

Being Fair

I know you are a kind person. I know you are kind because you took a child into your home who wasn't born to you and was unhealthy in some ways. You pledged to love them, teach them, and care for them. So I'm going to say with confidence that you are kind and you want to be fair.

I know you want to be fair. I know you try to be fair, but with an unwell child, you might end up feeling angry or resentful, when all you were really trying to do was be a good role model and be fair.

This is going to be hard for you.

Maybe two years down the road you can trust them to do the right thing, but for right now, life is not fair for them. This is for their healing and safety and the safety of other children, pets, and parents. If they had a seizure disorder, you wouldn't let them near strobe lights. In a similar way, they need you to be their filter, allowing in only what is safe and healthy for them. They will take advantage of almost any situation if they can. That will set back their healing and can cause a lot of resentment and retaliation in siblings.

It's hard to get love in and help your child heal when you are unhappy and the emotional climate in your house is topsy-turvy. Good boundaries will help everyone feel happier.

Your Child Is Just Having a Bad Day

You will run into bad days. Your child is naughty, sits okay, goes back to whatever, is naughty again—rinse and repeat. So this is just going to be a bad day. Your child probably needs some cuddly love time, but you may not be able to do that if you have other children or are working to a deadline or are just not in a great place yourself. So instead, you can have them pick out a few things to do and designate an area by you (say 6 feet by 6 feet) and say that they can play there today. You keep an eye on your child, of course, but usually your child is basically telling you they just can't handle things today. So you make it easy for them and put yourself more in charge.

No Spankings,

or angry lectures, or taking away food, or sending to their room, or withdrawing your love, no pulling hair, no grabbing ears, or vindictiveness, or revenge, or getting even, or imposing any kind of pain and suffering, or taking away an activity they love and are good at (and is good for them like soccer) … OH MY!!!

I almost didn't put this in because I personally think it goes without saying, but Layla had a way of getting under my skin and inciting rage. I am for sure guilty of some of these, and my husband was guilty of some of the others. Sometimes I would lock myself in a bathroom if I couldn't keep it together. Whatever you do, if you can't put a circle around your child (putting the limits on) and fill the circle with love as you let time make them a better person, then I haven't made the point of this book clear yet.

When your child just totally trashed their bedroom or sneakily put a hole in the living room wall, or does some other thing that really puts you into a rage, you say, "Come sit by me," have them sit by you, and wait it out until they are ready with their good sitting to be released. Then they really need to be monitored while they right their wrong or clean up their mess. Don't punish. Try to remember, your child has already been hurt far worse than a spanking, and you will never bind them with fear. Your "time-in" will work.

Before we met Doctor B., sometimes Layla would make sure she had my attention and then deliberately snap her hairbands to the breaking point. I liked to keep her hair tied back away from her face—and so she chose to express her rebellion by intentionally making her hair messy. It was a trigger that never failed to anger me. After I started doing time-ins, she still often did this behavior, but instead of an angry response, she got my smile. "Oh," I would tell her, "I see you want to come to sit by me for a while." She was testing the waters to see: *Is this new calmer Mom for real? How badly do I have to behave before the "screamer" comes back?* Expect a testing period when you start using the sit-by-me technique.

Think of it like this: Get them inside your circle and fill your circle only with love. Let time do the teaching.

Homeschooling? It Depends.

When Layla was four going on five, I decided I would teach her colors. This was before her diagnosis or the visit from Dr B. After a few weeks, she got every color in a book about colors correct except red and green. She could not seem to get those right. I even took her to an eye doctor to see if she was red/green color blind, as she had other vision problems. She was fine. Then another week or so went by, and I saw her reading the same book with my mother. She consistently got all the colors right! I was excited. The next time we went through the book together, we were upstairs in her bedroom. I was in a good place, and she seemed to be also—and yet, again, she couldn't recognize red and green. After a fair bit of time where I was getting more and more annoyed that she wouldn't say the colors right for me, I ended up grabbing the book, stomping out of her bedroom, and chucking the book down the stairs. This felt so good that I took every single book off her bookshelf and sent them flying down the stairs in twos and threes, yelling the whole time.

My son came to see what was going on and started to laugh (because evidently seeing his usually calm mother throw a colossal temper tantrum was the funniest thing he had ever seen)!

I was still mad and figured I had better get out of there or the bookshelf was going to be next.

As I sat outside by myself, with hot tears streaming down my face, my nose running, and no tissues, I could only dejectedly think, "What is wrong with me?"

Later, I learned that it was not my job to teach academic subjects to my child. My primary job was to teach her to accept my love. Most children are less defiant with their teachers, as they don't fear the heart connection with them, so go ahead and let teachers do their jobs while you do yours. If you really understand this and can get your child in a circle of your limits, fill that circle with love, and keep your heart in the right place, there is no problem with you running a homeschool program. But don't feel that you *have* to.

I did not homeschool. Layla went to a great public school where they got on board and trusted me to determine what was healthy and not healthy for my daughter, which left my morning and early afternoon hours free to run my business, get the grocery shopping done and spend time with my husband. When the kids got off the bus at 2:00, I was 100 percent focused to spend time with them. My daughter pretty much obeyed the rules with her teachers and other adults like her grandmother...Great! That meant I had people I could trust to leave her with and keep her healthy while I had other things to tend to. My time spent with her was slowly but surely healing that toughened little heart of hers. Ultimately, it's a personal decision, but homeschool only if you can do it without being angry and punitive. Homeschool only if you are really good at keeping a loving circle around your child and keeping them in it.

Your Child Doesn't Feel Well

In the beginning, I had energy and joy and wanted to teach Layla to walk, talk, and play like a typical child. In the middle of our journey, I started to worry and let fear and doubt sap my energy and commitment. When I realized she was heartsick or heartbroken, like a soldier with battle fatigue, and she needed special care from me, I was renewed and wanted to help her feel better. As time passed, I found that if I thought of Layla as "having an ouchy," I could be more compassionate and want to help her heal and feel better.

Babying Them (Reparenting)

This is important because it's a great way to fill your child's emotional piggy bank with quarters they don't even try to block. As often as you can, treat your child like they are three years younger than they are. I would say at least once a day.

If they are three years old, treat them to having bottles while cuddling with you and playing piggy-toe games.

If they are five years old, take different kinds of pudding and let them use their fingers to make designs on the table and then lick it off their hands.

If they want to be a baby horse, baby chick, baby anything, play along with finding them the proper bedding so they can "nest" (of course by you). You can even feed them appropriate food like carrots, fruit, and granola bars. These were items Layla would never eat for me at dinnertime, but she couldn't get enough of during playtime. Give them water or milk to lick out of a bowl.

Even into her teens, Layla still loved it if I asked her out of the blue, "Is that a baby kitten?" She never failed to say, "I'm the baby kitten!" Then play acted like she was a kitten. It became a silly, funny game we played for years.

After I learned that Layla needed mandatory love time, I swaddled her in blankets and gave her bottles and sang her songs. Our brains are hardwired to respond favorably to sweet milk, so I put two teaspoons of sugar in the bottles. Sometimes I felt awkward or silly treating a five-year-old like a little baby, but it was a sure-fire way to get love in while her guard was down. I have recently heard it called "reparenting"; I just know that even before she healed much, "babying" her would bring obvious delight.

For school-aged children, you can give them several caramel creams in the morning for them to put in their pocket. Make sure you tell them you filled them with special love from you and just for them. As they eat them throughout the day, the sugary center will stimulate their brain for bonding while you are apart.

Invest in a rocking chair!

Cuddly love time is mandatory every day for a successful outcome.

You must take time every day.

Even on bad days.

Get your heart in the right place and do it!

92

Resiliency

My mother is fond of saying, "Kids are resilient," and, "You worry too much. She will be fine." I have actually heard this from a lot of places and many different sources throughout my life.

I don't buy it.

Kids are young, they are fragile, they are without resources and reasoning. They are to be tended to with deliberation and care and softness and gentleness and butterfly kisses and soothing tones and bottles of sweet milk, until they drift off to sleep in your arms with enough trust that you will guide them and keep them safe.

Getting a Good Prognosis

Many mothers of children like Layla ask, "Do I need to be a stay-at-home mom?" It helps, but only if you can remain firm and loving throughout the day. I did stay at home because my husband and I owned our own business, which meant I could. I know this will sound drastic, but if your child has problems and they are younger than school age, if at all possible get your heart in the right place and stay at home.

If your child came from a hard place, the younger they are, the more easily they will bond. If you use the parenting principles I've described, you should have a good outcome.

Children age five or under usually have a good outcome. Those six to seven can heal, but it will probably be harder. Children eight to nine will be even harder. After age ten, Dr. B said he didn't think this approach would work as well. Other developmental stages will be starting at that point, which will make this program not as effective.

A good therapist experienced in attachment trauma should be able to help you find other or modified treatments for older children.

94

Shame

As Layla got older, she felt ashamed of her behavior from when she was little. She had good reason to feel ashamed, because before we got help, I sure shamed her many times for her behaviors. Even after I knew what was wrong and how to fix it, I had my own bad days and still shamed her.

I shamed her for breaking her toys, breaking her glasses, taking her pull-ups off, and wetting the bed. I shamed her for breaking her hair bands and her hair being a mess. I shamed her for acting dumb. I shamed her for being slow to get dressed or slow to get going and get in the car, I shamed her for being uncoordinated. I shamed her in general for just not being good enough.

I so wish I could take back every unkind word, pursed lip, tight look, frowning face, disgusted tone, rolled eye, huffy voice, sarcastic jibe, and impatient shove into a car seat, jacket sleeve, and high chair.

As parents, we tend to parent the way we were parented, and we have our own bad days. For a child with no trauma in their past, these parenting skills may be good enough to see us through. But a child with trauma in their past will most likely need you to acquire new skills and new ways of doing things. You will also need to become aware that parenting is having not only daily effects on you, your child, and your family, but also has long-reaching and lasting effects.

By far the hardest part . . .
my own heart.

96

I was pretty angry and resentful by the time we got our diagnosis that Layla was not bonding properly. At first, it was hard to change my parenting tactics and stay calm and in a good place. After the brush with the police, I had started thinking I might want to adopt Layla out of our family. I was afraid she would continue lying and that my husband or I might end up in jail someday. I thought she might actually succeed in tearing our family apart. It was the hardest thing I had to face in my life. I was depressed and scared.

When I understood I needed to change my parenting techniques and that she was never going to be like her brother or "spontaneously" bond to me . . . well, then I had to make an effort to be more loving and find attachment opportunities many times every day. That was actually the easier part for me. But getting her to obey my rules was harder for me. Layla had been pushing my buttons quite effectively for over two years, and I was pretty angry. If she needed a "time-in" because she had just done something out of bounds, it might have made me very angry and therefore hard to be loving. I couldn't effectively do a "time-in" if I was restraining myself from pulling her hair to get her into place or lecturing her while she was sitting there.

This only works when you have mastered your own heart. I suggest three things.

1. Give *yourself* a "time-in" when you are feeling upset: breathe, meditate, exercise, pray—basically whatever you need to do to calm down and pull yourself together.

2. Get a good individual therapist. Don't bother taking your child to therapy at this point, but for you, it's very helpful. You have your own hurts to work through, there may be times you need a cheerleader, and it will help keep you solid and on track.

3. Practice, and be patient with yourself. I was way better one year in than I was the first four months. After a time, Layla would spit on the floor, and I wouldn't miss a beat, saying, "Oops! Get a paper towel and clean that up please," and she did.

Getting Your Heart in the Right Place

Layla had been effectively pushing my buttons for years, and I was feeling angry, resentful, petty, cruel, and rejected. One professional I talked to said: "It's like Layla can't experience those emotions for herself, so she likes eliciting those emotions in you and then watching them play out."

Before any healing was able to take place I had to do a lot of my own work to get my heart into a loving, caring, and compassionate place.

Here are a few tools to help, if you have a little one at home who has been effectively pushing your buttons for months or years, and like me, compassion and a loving heart is not coming easily for you. These exercises are intended to help you put yourself in your child's place, so you can understand their reactions better. (Note that if your child's past trauma was not from being in an orphanage setting, you can adjust these exercises to match the actual situation.)

Exercise One—Eat a light breakfast and a light lunch. Have no snacks and no dinner. Go to bed and really take note of how you are feeling. Tired? Teary? Anxious? Crabby? How about uncared for? Unloved? Angry? Imagine you didn't know if you would be getting breakfast when you woke up the next morning.

Exercise Two—Put on a pair of tight pants or long shorts with no underwear. Sit in a bathtub so they are wet. Then take a thirty-minute walk without any socks on. As you take your walk notice how uncomfortable you are. Is your skin irritated or starting to develop a blister? How does it feel to have to keep walking? Do you want to quit early? Are you frustrated? Do you feel teary or angry? Imagine if there wasn't a thirty-minute time limit? Many toddlers sit in wet, soiled diapers for more than an entire day. Neglect is often unseen, but very damaging to a child's identity, feelings of self-worth and self concept. Over time, most neglected children get the message loud and clear that they are a bother and just not worth a caregiver's time, attention, and love.

Exercise Three—Fill your bathtub a third full of lukewarm water. Open the bathroom door so there is a draft. Without clothes on, completely submerge yourself in the water. Now just sit there, hair dripping wet, skin getting cold, for a minimum of fifteen minutes. Pretend you are a baby. Your caregiver has other babies to tend to on "bath day," and you are often left waiting for an unknown amount of time. You can't get yourself up and out of the water. You can't get yourself a dry towel and start to warm up. . . . Really let yourself feel how vulnerable you are. Crying will bring no help. As you wait, feel how cold you are getting, feel the discomfort of the dripping water on your skin. How do you feel? Sad? Lonely? Unloved? Frustrated? Then let those feelings go as you know having any feelings at all will not help you as you wait.

What have you learned from this? Maybe you never like to take baths and be clean? Maybe you feel depressed and helpless a lot of the time . . . maybe you feel resigned to the sense of worthlessness growing inside you. Many neglected and abused babies and toddlers feel like garbage kids on the inside, always waiting for someone to just throw them away. That is why they find it hard to trust any adult to take care of them.

The moment you are ready to quit is usually right before the moment the miracle happens. Don't give up!

It took a long while . . . maybe two years,
but finally I was able to cuddle and love
Layla without her pushing away.
I had more and more time
that was fun with Layla.
And then . . .

One day Layla's *spark* had become a strong, burning flame again! That's when Layla became warm on the inside! She was now a happy little girl! She smiled and laughed and made jokes and hugged me all the time. When she and I went walking, she always grabbed my hand and held on.

I was happy, and Layla was happy.

She smiled and laughed, had friends, and was physically and emotionally healthy. She even made jokes!

After a time and with practice, I was able to predict what would be hard for Layla and make her want to act out and push me away again. For example, always at the beginning and the end of the school year, we would go through a rough patch . . . and I would have to remind myself: *Layla has trauma and this trauma can be triggered at any time—like a soldier with battle fatigue.* Another trauma trigger would be the holidays and her birthday. I asked Dr. B why this was. He said that Layla still had trouble receiving love. That toughened little heart of hers could sometimes get tough again, and at the holidays and her birthday, with so much love pouring into her . . . well, she reverted back to that early defense mechanism.

When I took time to understand her, I only felt more love and compassion for the little sweetheart my daughter truly was.

Over time, I got used to Layla drawing beautiful pictures, asking me to play with her, and cuddling up with me to listen to stories. Once Layla was feeling better, she started learning her colors and numbers and animals—and everything else her teacher taught her!

I started realizing I loved how funny Layla was. I didn't have to make ways to spend time with her; I wanted to. Layla and I started laughing together. A LOT!

Thank goodness I never quit trying!!!

One day I came home from work and Layla had done a really good job cleaning the kitchen. She was excited and said, "Look, Mom! I cleaned the kitchen for you!"

With love in my heart and in my voice I said, "Aww Layla, you are such a good do-bee!"

"What am I?"

I hugged her and said again, "You are a good do-bee!"

Delighted, she literally buzzed around the house for a while.

Layla is an adult now. She has good friends, a passion for drawing, rides horses, enjoys word games, has a great sense of humor, knits and crochets, helps clean the house, and LOVES animals.

Layla is very sweet, very kind, very funny, and our whole family has been blessed and privileged to bear witness to the journey of her life so far.

It has been a long journey. I now know one thing for sure.

I am Layla's mother.

It turned out in the end that Layla was a sad, half-starved, lonely, cold, hungry, and above all, heartbroken little girl . . . but she still had a *spark*. Our love and rules were able to coax it into a strong, burning flame. A flame that Layla will have to keep her warm on the inside her whole life.

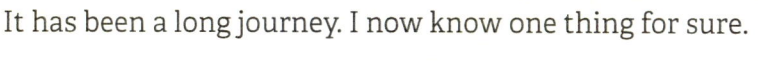

Amber Gregory is available to speak on trauma-informed parenting and keeping children safe from predators. For more information, contact:

AmberGregoryAuthor@gmail.com

or

www.learningtobelovedbook.com

SCAN ME

Amber Gregory is a mom, author, and passionate advocate for children who have faced trauma. Her first book, *Little Sweetheart,* shares her own journey of healing after sexual abuse, and her second, *Learning to Be Loved,* explores how adoptive families can help children rediscover trust and connection.

A seminary student at Drew University, Amber is pursuing her master's in theology and ministry, following her call to serve foster and adoptive families with compassion and hope. She speaks and teaches on topics like grooming, the cycle of abuse, and healing attachment wounds—always with the goal of helping children feel safe and deeply loved.

Amber believes that love, education, and inclusiveness can transform lives. Whether through her books, workshops, or conversations with parents, she continues to shine a light on how families can build bonds that heal.

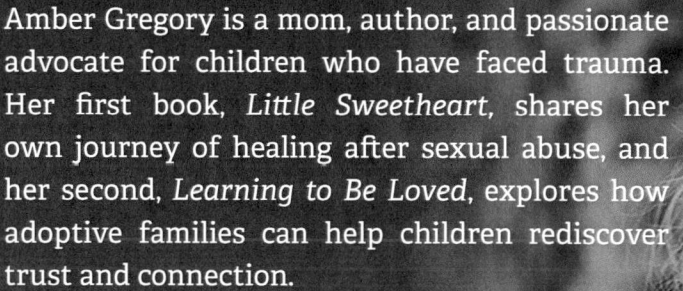

Further Reading on These Topics

Healing Parents: Helping Wounded Children Learn to Love & Trust
by Michael Orlans and Terry M. Levy

Close Time by Walter D. Buenning

Autonomy Circles by Walter D. Buenning

Spoiled Child Syndrome by Walter D. Buenning

The Connected Parent by Lisa Qualls and Karyn Purvis, PhD

Beyond Consequences, Logic, and Control by Heather Forbes and Bryon Post

Logic and Control by Bryon Post

When Love Is Not Enough: A Guide to Parenting with Reactive Attachment Disorder
by Nancy Thomas

The Heart and the Bottle by Oliver Jeffers

Why a Daughter Needs a Mom by Gregory E. Lane

You Taught Me to Love by Misty Black

Attachment, Trauma, and Healing by Terry Levy and Michael Orlans

The Body Keeps the Score: Brain, Mind and Body in the Healing of Trauma
by Bessel VanDerKolk, MD

Some Definitions from the American Psychiatric Association's *Diagnostic and Statistical Manual of Mental Disorders*, Edition 5 (DSM-5)

RAD

The DSM-5 lists Reactive Attachment Disorder (RAD) under Trauma and Stress-Related Disorders and gives the following definition and criteria:

A. A consistent pattern of inhibited, emotionally withdrawn behavior toward adult caregivers, manifested by both of the following:

    1. The child minimally seeks comfort when distressed.

    2. The child rarely or minimally responds to comfort when distressed.

B. A persistent social and emotional disturbance characterized by at least two of the following:

    1. Minimal social and emotional responsiveness to others.

    2. Limited positive affect.

    3. Episodes of unexplained irritability, sadness, or fearfulness that are evident even during nonthreatening interactions with adult caregivers.

C. The child has experienced a pattern of extremes of insufficient care as evidenced by at least one of the following:

    1. Social neglect or deprivation in the form of persistent lack of having basic emotional needs for comfort, stimulation and affection met by adult caregiving adults.

    2. Repeated changes of primary caregivers that limit opportunities to form stable attachments. (e.g., frequent changes in foster care).

3.   Rearing in unusual settings that severely limit opportunities to form selective attachment (e.g., institutions with high child to caregiver rations).

D.   The care in Criteria C is presumed to be responsible for the disturbed behavior in Criteria A (e.g. the disturbances in Criteria A began following lack of adequate care in Criterion C.)

E.   The criteria are not met for autism spectrum disorder.

F.   The disturbances are evident before age 5 years.

G.   The child has a developmental stage of at least 9 months.

ODD

The DSM-5 lists Oppositional Defiant Disorder (ODD) under Disruptive, Impulse Control, and Conduct Disorders and gives the following definition and criteria:

A.   A pattern of angry/irritable mood, argumentative/defiant behavior, or vindictiveness lasting at least 6 months as evidenced by at least four symptoms of the following categories, and exhibited during interaction with at least one individual who is not a sibling:

Angry/Irritable Mood

1.   Often loses temper

2.   Is often touchy or easily annoyed

3.   Is often angry and resentful

Argumentative/Defiant Behavior

4.   Often argues with authority figures or, for children and adolescents, with adults

5. Often actively defies or refuses to comply with requests from authority figures with rules

6. Often deliberately annoys others

7. Often blames others for his or her mistakes or misbehavior

Vindictiveness

8. Has been spiteful or vindictive at least twice within the past 6 months.

Note: The persistence and frequency of these behaviors should be used to distinguish a behavior that is within normal limits from a behavior that is symptomatic. For children younger than 5 years, the behavior should occur on most days for a period of at least 6 months unless otherwise noted (Criterion AB). For individuals 5 years or older, the behavior should occur at least once per week for at least 6 months unless otherwise noted (Criterion AB). While these frequency criteria provide guidance on a minimal level of frequency to define symptoms, other factors should also be considered, such as whether the frequency and intensity of the behaviors are outside a range that is normative for the individual's developmental level, gender, and culture

B. The disturbance in behavior is associated with distress in the individual or others in his or her immediate social context. (e.g., family, peer group, work colleagues), or impacts negatively on social, educational, occupational, or other important areas of functioning.

C. The behaviors do not occur exclusively during the course of a phychotic, substance use, depressive, or bipolar disorder. Also, the criteria are not met for disruptive mood dysregulation disorder.

CD-Childhood Onset Type

The DSM-5 lists Conduct Disorder (CD): Childhood Onset Type under Disruptive, Impulse Control, and Conduct Disorders and gives the following definition and criteria:

A. A repetitive and persistent pattern of behavior in which the basic rights of others or major age-appropriate societal norms or rules are violated, as manifested by the presence of at least three of the following 15 criteria in the past 12 months from any of the categories below, with at least one criterion present in the past 6 months:

Aggression to People and Animals

1. Often bullies, threatens, or intimidates others.

2. Often initiates physical fights.

3. Has used a weapon that can cause serious physical harm to others (e.g., a bat, brick, broken bottle, knife, gun).

4. Has been physically cruel to people.

5. Has been physically cruel to animals.

6. Has stolen while confronting a victim (e.g., mugging, purse snatching, extortion, armed robbery).

7. Has forced someone into sexual activity.

Destruction of Property

8. Has deliberately engaged in fire setting with the intention of causing serious damage.

9. Has deliberately destroyed others' property (other than by fire setting).

Deceitfulness or Theft

10. Has broken into someone else's house, building, or car.

11. Often lies to obtain goods or favors or to avoid obligations (i.e., "cons" others).

12. Has stolen items of nontrivial value without confronting a victim (e.g., shoplifting, but without breaking and entering; forgery).

Serious Violations of Rules

13. Often stays out at night despite parental prohibitions, beginning before age 13 years.

14. Has run away from home overnight at least twice while living in the parental or parental surrogate home, or once without returning for a lengthy period.

15. Is often truant from school, beginning before age 13 years.

B. The disturbance in behavior causes clinically significant impairment in social, academic, or occupational functioning.

C. If the individual is age 18 years or older, criteria are not met for antisocial personality disorder.

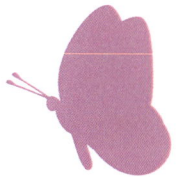

If you found this book useful, please help others learn about attachment and bonding by leaving a review.

Also by Amber Gregory
Little Sweetheart: How I Healed After Sexual Abuse
—and How You Can Protect Other Children from Grooming and Abuse

Publisher: Anamchara Books

www.ingramcontent.com/pod-product-compliance
Lightning Source LLC
Chambersburg PA
CBRC090838120626
46551CB00008B/692